Animals in Fall

Published by The Child's World®
1980 Lookout Drive • Mankato, MN 56003-1705
800-599-READ • www.childsworld.com

Photographs ©: Shutterstock Images, cover, 1, 5, 10–11,
16–17; Bonnie Taylor Barry/Shutterstock Images, 6; Eric
Wang/Shutterstock Images, 9; Tom Reichner/Shutterstock
Images, 13, 15; Yuval Helfman/Shutterstock Images,
18; Margaret M. Stewart/Shutterstock Images, 21

Design Element: Shutterstock Images

ISBN 9781503816596
LCCN 2016945909

Printed in the United States of America
PA02323

ABOUT THE AUTHOR
Jenna Lee Gleisner is an author
and editor from Minnesota. Her
favorite part about fall is the
changing colors.

Contents

Time to Prepare

It is fall. A squirrel **gathers** as many nuts as it can.

Animals **prepare** in fall. Winter is coming. Soon there will be no new food to eat.

Bears eat a lot. They build fat. Fat will keep them warm. They sleep all winter.

Snakes find shelter.
They find **burrows**
or old logs.

Changes

Deer grow long hair. The hair will keep them warm in winter.

The fur of some animals changes color. A brown snowshoe hare turns white. It will blend in with winter snow.

Find Warmer Weather

Some animals leave.

Geese fly south.

It is warmer there.

Monarch butterflies fly south too. This **swarm** goes to Mexico.

All animals prepare.

Soon winter will be here.

Monarch Butterfly Craft

Make a monarch butterfly!

Supplies:

paper   orange paint
black marker   paper plate

Instructions:

1. Take the black marker. Draw a thick black line on your paper. This is the butterfly's body.

2. Squirt paint on a paper plate.

3. Press both hands in the paint. Make sure the palms of your hands are covered in paint. Make two handprints on each side of the body. This makes the wings.

4. Let the paint dry. Take the black marker. Draw lines and spots on the wings.

Glossary

burrows — (BUR-ohz) Burrows are tunnels or holes in the ground made or used as homes for animals. In fall, snakes find burrows to stay in.

gathers — (GATH-urz) When an animal gathers, it collects things. A squirrel gathers nuts in fall so that it will have food to eat during the winter.

prepare — (pri-PAIR) To prepare is to get ready. In fall, animals prepare for the winter.

swarm — (SWORM) A swarm is a large group of people or insects that moves together. A swarm of butterflies flew south together.

To Learn More

Books

Felix, Rebecca. *What Do Animals Do in Fall?* Ann Arbor, MI: Cherry Lake Publishing, 2013.

Herrington, Lisa M. *How Do You Know It's Fall?* New York, NY: Children's Press, 2014.

Web Sites

Visit our Web site for links about fall animals: **childsworld.com/links**

Note to Parents, Teachers, and Librarians: We routinely verify our Web links to make sure they are safe and active sites. So encourage your readers to check them out!

Index